10 PLUS ONE

Poems by

Ann Kammerer

with one by Jill

For Jill and Eric.

10 PLUS ONE

CONTENTS

These poems were built on things my little daughter said. I wrote the first 10 to encourage her to write. She wrote the last one to encourage me to write, too.

10 POEMS

● ● ● ● ● ● ● ● ● ●

One night rhyme

You remember
Then forget
The clock ticks
You sleep.

They say
Dreams are made
In the night before day.
So you awake
Peeking from the sheets
To see if that's real.

But it's dark
Shadows crawl
On the wall.
Nearby
Your dog sleeps.
Her breathing tuned
To your heart.

They say
Night becomes day
And day becomes night
So you wait
Your eyes eclipsed
As you tumble back to sleep.

●

Almost snow

The day fades
And within the gray
You see
Bright yellow flowers
Their petals
Arcing like sparks
To the sky.

Your hands
Once warm
Feel cold.
So new.
So sharp.
Like ice.

So you walk
Stirring the leaves
That burst in crimson
And fall like flames
Through the thin almost snow.

Where are you sun?

You wake up and look out
On a morning so dark
And so different
Than yesterday.

Just then it was bright.
And your dog
Slept in a warm spot
On the floor.

Where are you sun?
You tap the window but it's dark.
The white snow gray
Against the black.

Where are you sun?
You tap again and something rises
Round and gold
In the morning sky.

There you are sun . . .
And it's bright.
So bright.
Splashing the sky
With a yellow glaze
That melts the cool white snow.

● ● ●

Being sick, being well

The best thing
They say
About being sick
Is feeling good
When you're well.

But you know that.
You remember the day
You awoke
Your hair still damp
From a fever
Your skin not sore
To the touch.

Your room was cold
But you got up.
By the window
Your skin reflected
The blue morning light
As your fingertips melted
The frost on the panes.

● ● ● ●

Blue no more

The blue ends
When it meets the green
A sky
A hill
With thin bare trees.

The gray uncurls
To divide the yellow
A road
A field
With dry brittle grass.

So you walk
Leaving the sun
That warms your back.
Clouds hang in slivers
Some purple
Some pink
Fading to wisps.

But it's day
Until the blue turns to black
Speckled with stars
And a moon
That pierces the sky.

Holes in velvet

The sky changes
From the palest blue
To indigo
Then to a black
As deep and pure
As white.

Between a slice of moon
Stars sparkle
Scattered holes in velvet
That bring signs of light
From the other side.

The judge's pool

There are four chairs
Around the judge's pool.
You can see them
Through the black iron fence.
Red, blue, green and yellow.
They're bright
And empty.
No one is ever there.

Except on days
When you walk by.
His fuzzy dogs yap
As you hold hands
With your mom.

What's wrong you say.
And when you speak
They stop.
Wagging their tails
Their tongues curl
As they slip back
To lie poolside
Their smooth white fur
Glistening like ghosts.

When the tree fell

The clearness came
When the tree fell
A sky so different
Pale
Unblemished
And blue.

Two men
Misty with dust
Wiped their faces.
Bird flitted
In angry chatter
Then flew away.

Darn birds one said.
Darn birds said the other.
Smiling
They kicked the trunk
And sawed again.

Up above
The sky spread like paper
Untouched
Unfolded
The stillness etched
By a skinny cloud.

● ● ● ● ● ● ● ●

Someplace real

You pick a place
That's real
Someplace
With sun
And water
That laps the sand
With emeralds.

We'll stay there
You say
Until we're warm
Cooled by trees
With leaves like blades
That never fall.

It's a place
You say
Not far
From the flame.
And outside
Ice forms from rain
And falls in sheets
That slice the sky.

● ● ● ● ● ● ● ● ●

Perception

Some see the world
In black and white
Others in shades
Perceiving realities
Clear and unclear
Distinctly different
Than defined.

Up or down
Big or small
The world turns
Second by second
Minute by minute
Every 24 hours
Until complete.

● ● ● ● ● ● ● ● ● ●

PLUS ONE

● ● ● ● ● ● ● ● ● ●
●

My pen

My pen . . .
Just sitting there
Waiting to write
For its end to go "snap"
And its ink to splash out
On the paper.
My pen.
My beautiful pen.

ABOUT THE AUTHOR

Ann Kammerer is a professional writer who lives in Michigan with her husband Eric and daughter Jill.

ABOUT JILL

Jill lives with her parents and just finished fourth grade. She likes reading, playing guitar and piano, dancing and swimming, and hanging out with her friends.

●

Made in United States
Orlando, FL
07 May 2023

32895369R00022